OF TEA, TANTRUMS AND TALES

SYED NAHIDA ANJUM

Copyright © Syed Nahida Anjum
All Rights Reserved.

This book has been published with all efforts taken to make the material error-free after the consent of the author. However, the author and the publisher do not assume and hereby disclaim any liability to any party for any loss, damage, or disruption caused by errors or omissions, whether such errors or omissions result from negligence, accident, or any other cause.

While every effort has been made to avoid any mistake or omission, this publication is being sold on the condition and understanding that neither the author nor the publishers or printers would be liable in any manner to any person by reason of any mistake or omission in this publication or for any action taken or omitted to be taken or advice rendered or accepted on the basis of this work. For any defect in printing or binding the publishers will be liable only to replace the defective copy by another copy of this work then available.

Contents

Contents

1. Disturbances

The crushed grapes stained my chipped nails
The sun got more lonely one tiring afternoon
My parched eyes scanned the stunned courtyard
My shoes hurt me, suffocating my feet
The corner of my kitchen felt freezing, marble cold
Lifeless, frozen skin, unfocused frenzy eyes
High pitched laughter demanded a lavish meal
The bleeding tomatoes and my scrapped elbows
I cooked lots for them, toxic herbs, bottled potions
The tap leaked filling the sink, flooding the kitchen
I drowned in finger licking soups
Soups that you ate with your hands
We had food from cans , rotten mouldy stuff
The dead fish swam in the tap water
The skeletons with borrowed wings, pest flies
The dinner table caught fire, roasted feats
We had tap water soups, sprinkled with crushed grapes
Crushed grapes that stained my nails
We headed to sleep with empty stomachs
So then they drank infested waters and extracted threads
Cut quilts, feather less pillows, threadbare carpets
And now we went to sleep with full stomachs
The man in a white suit, inviting instruments

They shut the door; he lit a cigarette, smoke
My eyes focused on the rings, he fished for another
Then another, he smoked and inhaled
The last one, then we searched for it
I fed him crushed grapes that stained my nails
And they never knew....

2. My cup of tea

Brew me a beverage with some extra cardamom
For the whiff itself will serve as a my time machine
And transport me back to that frosty day
When frostbites were your guests for that year
But my red chilled nose mattered more
Some extra leaves and your mother's most expensive spices
Bubbled and brewed, and then melted
Everything inside me If not the love but some extra spices
Can you still put them in my cup of tea?

3. Wild

Dragon hides clothed her
Phoenix feathers decorated her hair
Wildflowers scented her
Gushing Brooks bathed her
Dragon fire warmed her
Stars served as security
The moon as the lamp
Nymphs entertained her
And the trees fanned her
Burning dandelions served as Aurora
And the whole sky as the ceiling
Fruits feasted her
Animals always at a call
Birds were the messengers
And then one day
The mortals took her
Made her
Fall in love with them
Gave her responsibility
Taught her rules
Gave her opinions
Hurt her
Then left her

Being alone was what she had grew up with
But it was a different loneliness
Like a heavy crowded emptiness
And then
Her hair hung loose
Dirty, coiled wires
Skin scratched
Cut lips
Bloodshot eyes
But she laughed
Manic?
Nope, it was funny
Hilarious
And they called the woods wild......

4. Dead Melodies

The old radio blared on in the background
Sometimes I just want to press the stop button
Then maybe even the rewind button
Then the play button once again Stop. Go back. Play and on
and on
The atmosphere hung heavy in there
Of dullness. Of emptiness. Of nothingness
But still too heavy, way too heavy
Chairs seemed to be pressed under it
Under the unmanageable weight
The heavy heaviness, the empty presence
When no one was present there
And that is what made it too crowded
Visitors that never rang the doorbell
Hands that never touched the knocker
Fingers that never pressed the light switches
Feet that never crossed the threshold
Voices that never did away with the silence
Still the absence witnessed some presence
That fine layer of dust over the embroidered cushions
Those cobweb covered curtains and ceilings
Dead insects dangling from the chandeliers
Puffs of dust in the carpets, though yet to be blown

That mould covered splendid meal, greasy pots and pans
But now they were used to it, to everything of it
To the heavy absence, to the weird presence
To those lonely gusts of air that came in
Through the unattended nooks and comers, the crevices
To The lonely drops of water that the heavy rainfall granted
To the longing for the visitor that never visited
To how there silent screaming was never heard
To how they were granted nothing at all
Neither the understanding nor the misunderstanding
But now they have learned, a great deal actually
Not how to live with it , but how everything is in vain
But did that make them stop ever?
Stop waiting?
Stop wailing?
Stop watching?
The music sounded so dead now
As if a composition from some graveyard
As if it came from the dead, the gone
As if from the visitor that never visited...

5. Bride

Threads of shimmering golden thread sewn into the outlandish exotic flowers. A never seen before shade of melting orange tinted stone encrusted in the middle of blooming satin petals. A repetition of the patterns of celebration. The clocks witnessing the spending of the threads, the miniature stones. The ceaseless waves of the sea of fabrics. A tapestry of the put in effort, the awaiting moments, the gazing through mosaic glass splattered panes , the racing of the little fluttering heart, the humongous change in the monotonous destiny.

Reclining over the plush couches of royal pastels, the long tresses winded into delicate knots of ancient culture, they all awaited for the token of her special day. With a threshold waiting for her to cross over, she reclined headlong, henna laden palms facing upwards , over the turquoise velvet couch placed at the core of anticipation . Under the clash of suggestions of wearing the many satins and silks hanging in walnut vaults, the princess lifted her head and let the waterfall of her dark royal cocoa hair shower the shoulders resting at her waist. The anticipation fogged eyes looked at the gigantic metal studded door. The quivering lips slightly parted, a doorway to slow dizzy gasps of air. The flick of the coco waterfall disturbing the set pattern of the still air, the princess dragged her feet to welcome what was yet to arrive. Where were the ladies bearing the trays? The engraved trays carrying the messages of joys yet to come. Bearing the heavy fabrics dyed with shades available in no bazaars. The right shade conjured by the artist under the veil of one lazy forgotten afternoon in an ambitious studio. The cottages of a thousand shades of a few colours. An orchestra of obscure instruments sweeten the air all around. And all that the imagination links with moments of happiness do start to take shape hidden behind the air. Heavenly urns pouring in the melody rendering the atmosphere vibrantly musical. The women glide in bearing in the trays sparking up the celebrations as the doors open a wide ajar. Attend to the princess like never before. Her royal self can no more behold the tumultuous joy inside her. Seen from a bird's view, it is a Sufi dance of ecstasy. Unwrapped from what was held on to reluctantly and wrapped in what feels like a deserved moment of victory. The princess's veil helps her to glide in the space in between with utter elegance.

She stands there like a picture made with the finest combination of brush strokes. The delicate fingers brushing the deep carvings of the necklace wrapping her delicate neck. The Kohl sprinkled eyelashes cast down. A strand of cocoa hair slipping onto the face. A laugh sounding like the tinkling noise of the fairies of the lost hills. She is looking like the beautiful chaos that crept into her mind and stood there determined, the rest will follow just fine….!

6. Flickering Lights

Against the moss covered crumbling wall
I rested my weary, dirty blonde head
The nearest tree was bare, poverty stricken
And so were all the seemingly homeless trees
But the moss grew like a parasite
On the red shingles of the deserted house
On the cold marble stairs I rested myself upon
A slight breeze came as an intruder
Making the bare branches compose a creepy tone
Like skeletons having a dead dance party
The bones tapping too hard, the joints popping too fast
The cold panes seemed to glare at me
The cold marble eyes, the bodiless sight
It wouldn't look away, my rejection of no use
I got up, breaking the ice, cutting the chill
The cold day made the leaves swirl, dance
Around my feet, bronze with brown, rust with red
All shades mingling, colourful horrors
Gathering my jacket more tightly around myself
I headed another way, but the chill accompanied me
A knot of little fells passed by me
High pitched laughter, blindingly coloured woollens
But nothing coloured the cold creeping chills

All colours fading into black, white and gray zones
The olive fence creaked open
The shrubs looked strangely uninviting
Another gust of wind, strange airs
The day nature went into a coalition with horrors
Rain splattered windows trembled with the shutting of the
door
That winter I had spent on the dishes
Rose patterned, dandelion designed plates
Mustard painted, rust shaded teapots
But nothing added colour, not a thing felt cheery
The gloom seemed to veil all the crockery, the things

Dark, dingy, cobweb laden corners
No brooms, no brushes got them clean now
The webs seemed stuck stubbornly
The stained sink was blocked, not again
The tap dripped uncontrollably, plink-plink-plink
The sole lamp flickered on and off
The wets overwhelming, the lights deceiving
The sickening chipped green phone rang shrilly
"Hello, who is that? The voice came hollow
"You still there? Still alive?" chilling chorus
"What? What do you mean?" breathlessness
"You exceeded the time limit", lazy drawl
"What?' dizziness
"Never mind, it was never too late', chilling confidence

And the sole flickering lamp went out.

7. Holiday

Novel mornings, the exciting alarms
The locks wanting to dance to their tunes
Turkish fez, the wavering melodies
The goose bumps became regular visitors
Extra sprinkle of cinnamon, hot cocoa
The labelling as the coffee girl
Lost track time, welcomed merging
The dance in strange lands to strange songs
Frenzy plans, spontaneous adventures
The warm touch of the bonfires
Roasted marshmallows, open fire roasts
The snug sleeping bags under the starry sky
Once in a while I fetch my dream catcher
And set to catch my wandering dreams
I leap over mountains, swim the vast seas
Collecting the fuel for my bland days...

8. The unwanted guest

There is this continuous humming

Back there, in my skull, my mind

I never was a warm host

I served it colds pies and soggy chips

But it liked to feed on the stale, I guess

Then one fine morning

I hung a warning, from a weakening vine

'No visitors allowed, to be left in peace'

Loopholes were its speciality, the smart song

Accompanying one of them, it made an entry

A very unwelcome guest, an imposter

The irony though was the determination

A cart full of its luggage

Mattresses and mints, quills and quilts, parchment and potions

He had come for a long visit

Depression and dampness, horror and hopelessness

The dark magician carries the abstract too

And the worst of all is that evil flute of his

Full of holes, holes that never made recovery, never were filled

Dripping blood, dripping hopes... happiness

That tip- tap...tip- tap...that horrifying tune

That humming in the back of my mind

How hard I try to have my house back
"I never came for some time , I am by your side forever"
He walks around like he owns the place
Playing his flute, dripping darkness everywhere
Sprays, herbs and incense have been rendered useless
The stink, the dampness, the darkness prevails everywhere
You will learn to live with it, give it some time
Do away with the lanterns, the hopes, the happiness
True to my sign, nothing visits me now
But no one knows about this secret visitor of mine
How he never leaves me now
A carriage passed by, full of folks
"Oh! This one is a loner, never out of the house"
"Never liked people, you know such lot"
And then it drove away fast, escaping almost
No fist hammered the bolted door
Leaving behind puffs of dust and also the loner

9. Lemons and the dead

There is a lot to ask myself
Where do I begin?
The frilly curtains are fluttering fast
I can hear the tap open
Sometimes I wish I could just sink
Sink in my overfilled bathtub
Then I left it open overnight
And it just filled and filled and filled
Sometimes I wish weird
Does that make me weird?
You don't need to answer that
I understand, see I have frilly curtains too
That day I thought I was dreaming
So I picked the many lemons
And called it a day
But then the next day
I realised we had only lemon trees
So I got angry and upset
With my dead as a doornail gardener
Though he never forgets to whisper
From his graveyard somewhere in my garden
A token of gratitude, I have flowers all over
Do I wonder too much? Sometimes I wonder

What if one day I could no more
That is a weird thing to say; sleep paralysis
We have an odd combination of colours
We painted our kitchen with striking colours
Revolting colour and then lost our appetites
I still had an appetite though
I am not weird you know
But I drowned my food in milk
And they believed and were deceived
Then I had a bath in my drowning bathtub
And watched me from deep below
That wavering face that leered from above...

10. Downpour

When the leaves seemed at war
The air finally made itself felt
When the dark era seemed to have taken over
You stood by the window
Peeping hard, peering through
Daylight merged into darkness
The boundaries got unclear, hazy
Is there a storm coming?
The darkness before the downpour
Hydro spheres intersecting the atmosphere
The letting go of work
Raindrops sliding your collarbone
The distant hooting of some bird
Music to your reading
To time travel
Drizzle
Little hands shaping paper boats
Frogs having one of their days
Chocolate puddles
The dance under the vast sky
Granny's lined buckets
The weeping canopies
Downpour

Rushing to your house
Crackling fires, drying socks
Plastic boots, wet umbrellas
Standing under strange roofs
Heads under wet wings
Raining cats and dogs
Nostalgic feelings
The dynamics of water!

11. Faces

My bedside lights flooded the room hazy
I hid under the coloured, aged lights
I heard the front door open, the thud
The bells I had hung from the nails
Clink, thud footsteps, umbrella on the stand
She had come late today, she was tired
So I took out the cold denim, the rough soles
So I categorise myself, a messy perfectionist
They taught her so much, then also the ride home
I tried to suppress my laughter, I didn't understand a thing
The morning professor, her tired coffee bores me
Lazy drinks leave her tired, sleeping skins
I will go to bed early today, ogling night owls
They had planned of burying me under the papers today
I will work faster, spilling ink, papers with holes
Beyond the window pane, she visits the supermarket
I love her curls, housework never effected her
Autumn winds mess with my garden flora
I sweep the garden clean, harsh winds
Harsh winds crack his lips, brute airs
Puffs of steam, boiling waters, homemade moisturizers
He will be fine, she tells him to dress warm
I glanced outside the window again, partly seeing

Signatures, stamps, orders and the wait at the dinner table

My kitchen clocks move faster when I am out

Cleaning dishes I don't eat from, spotless dirty dishes

I look at the clock and I am late again

Bristle moustached boss never allows me to leave early

The kitchen fire makes me doze off and I wait for him

He knocks the door, the night air froze me

I had dinner with me, he ate with gusto

The morning professor frightens me though

My assignments in the cold denim pocket

The food tastes bland, my senses have dimmed

The light flickers off, the crevice the darkness came in through

The darkness, the lullabies, the sliding into dreams

The scribbling takes my night away, I don't sleep tonight

Scribbled notes, bland dinners, piling files

The day the boss finally gave a day off

The day when no dinners had to be cooked

The day the term finally ended

My salty hair flies, my skin is all tanned

I laugh with the scorching sun, the kissing sand

And then I dive in my refreshing cup of tea

But I never hit the bottom though

One day the sun shone bright

The palm trees swayed for a week

And then I left....

12. Freedom

Freedom frightens me now
It stretches like endless hollowness
A tunnel with no light at its end
Lets my mind be a wanderer
Visit places it could never visit
Dream dreams that never fulfill
Feel feelings that shouldn't be felt
Hope for hopeless hopes
Freedom bearing innumerable chains
Freedom luring into sweet captivity
Freedom an essence, an abstract idea
Captivity set me limitless limits
Assured me, I was safe and sound
Within its periphery, within confinement
When freedom sets me loose, be alone
I seek for captivity, for security within limitations
Broken wings end my expectations
Make me want less, keeping my heart safe
Endless flights breaking barriers
Fluttering heart, high hopes, ray of sunshine
But then the dusk seemed too near
The sun set too quickly, defying laws
Empty vessels, deafening noises

Dampened souls and a broken heart
Yeah. It broke my heart. Tore it apart
But then also the heart, cleverly cunning
Knowing that it doesn't belong with me
Wanting it more than any other possession
A possession metamorphosing into obsession
Lumps in my throats left me too
I don't even have a vent now
How dead can you be when you are alive?
No one answers that for me: freedom credited
Body supporting a shawl of love
Heart an extinguished lamp
A constant ache, my incense
Cross my boundary and it seeps in
But this one thing is mine

All things unwanted are mine
All the aches, the hurts, the disappointments
My wonderland drove me crazy
I alone was driven to madness
Madly in love, insanely shattered
I don't want to be among the nice, the mad
A toast to my normalcy my utopia
"I love it", says the normal girl
"All yours", comes back the reply
Let my utopia be reality for once
But in that cruel prevailing background

"Little girl, reality is just an illusion"
And the little heart broke yet once again.

13. Abstract jeering

Overlapping designs, intricate patterns, weird doodles

One salty tear rolled down my jaw line

The common struggles of generations

The achievable victories too, I got up

"But I ate you yesterday too"

"Aha! Mockery at its best"

"My many lives", brushing the crumbs away

The class of it, so gentle...toasty

Subconscious, sleepy replies, clumsy archery

"I ate you, chewed you like chew chew,

Crumbled you, then gulped you, then..."

"Well whatever...I am here once more"

When carbs got egoistic

Intolerable talking, so I eat you up too

Somewhere far away, a family conversed

Faint voices, faint goodbyes, faint reminding of left things

Well I don't complain, I have a birdie too

'Cuckoo, cuckoo, time to get out"

The clocks chocked on their laughter

"Sleepyhead loves his bed

His eyes, a sleepy red

One day he slept too much, they said

And then they discovered him dead"

The strings vibrated all together
And then the guitar winked at me
Frustrations got me fetching for the uniform
My brand new mirror captured me
"Hola! Ah my reflection stinks"
If only mirrors could run
"You are my reflection not me...both are me"
"Both are you, prisoner to lifelessness"
Something is chocking me, tied ties
And then the perfect knots knotted me
It was cloudy near the shoe rack
Nobody wanting to drag the sleepyhead
Through the gravel, slippery marbles
And ito the paper scented office
Ah! The dullness of it
The brown pointed to the black
The black pointed to the brown
They bonded over the canvas
The canvas played it cool, reservation for holidays
The reluctance and the lock clicked
Through the letterbox, a sigh of relief
Ah! This house sickens me
Same here
Finally things made sense
I started the car and heard the noise
Over the growling engine
"Can you please drive properly today?

Ah! The fed up drawl....

14. Travel

Intricate designs of my tunic fascinated me
The glint of my nose ring holding me still
A wisp of hair supporting a rainbow of shades
Cramel, Chocolate, dark forest, Gothic candy
Red flags fluttering hard in the breeze
Fluttering never being the same as tearing apart
UV repellent eye wear always at my service
Soles worn out despite many yellow cabs
New revelations to my taste buds every moment
Sweets never savoured before, flavours never felt before
A bohemian blend of tastes and flavours
Ceaseless roads, inception of endless architecture
Never knew that many shades of red before
Not red, neither maroon, a zip zap boom colour in between
Nature behaving as a stranger too
Striking sunrises, surprising sunsets
Weird waters, alluring airs
More in depths I dive, more perplexed I get
Puzzling over the problem, getting me bemused...bewildered
Travelling means freedom, so relish even getting lost
Lost in the alluring airs, tropical trees, outlandish ornaments
So let the ticking of the clock witness you
Tightening your backpack straps

Grabbing the dust laden map
And finally leaving your hobbit hole for once
For who did never looked back again
And moving on is not a bad thing after all...

15. Memories

Colourful delicate threads intertwine
In these dancing fingers of mine
Rippling waters adore my ankles
Young buds perfume the hair tresses
Let one day be set free for feelings
All of them let them wash me over
And then witness me emerge free
Like the free soul I have always been
A jar full of soft small stones
Embroidered by the salty waves
A jar full of fully felt feelings
I get to choose one...nostalgia
And then I took the train back
Starry nights and that huge lonely tree
Was enough to give you chills
Make you have your veggies quietly
The darkness reflecting window at night
Enough to keep you expecting for a ghost
Granny making sure to emphasize the appearance
Long nails, long dishevelled hair and the strange feet
The prison your home became on a Sunday morning
And the school bell at the end of a day
Your personal light at the end of the tunnel

The brook beside your old cottage

Your favourite fishing spot in summer

Being fishless never mattered

Holding the old rods was enough

Enough to transcend all physical boundaries

Your fluffy cotton candy clouds

Your rod catching the stars, the dreams

When sacrifices really mattered, too much actually

"Cutting my hair, if I got the score'

"Bathing everyday if I got the bike"

Wishes and self satisfying baits Ah!

Well...chubby cheeks, dimpled chin

Bargaining brats, demons within

Eyes are blue, lovely too

Dear tooth fairy, is that you??

The milky, thirty two, the fangs

Crumbling memory, reality, utopia

The train goes back and fro

Searching the lost stations

But then the track ended

The flag fluttered in the stinging air

Back to the present, to now

If only memories were beach pebbles

I would have played the game everyday

But then also it is just theoretical physics

Time travel never travelled to beaches

16. Greek love

Moonlight falling on my face whispered beautiful

But then in the blanket of darkness, even nature can just be an illusion

My silver orb don't mimic the mortal for it reduces me to nothingness and then you flood my nights every night

And then for even Narcissus, his love mirrored a sieve

Each time he tried to touch it, the ripples it preferred

They say Echo watched his decline resentfully but was then moved to pity

But even that one moment of resentment didn't cross my threshold

Death will be a cure quoted Narcissus but won't the soul still live on?

And your absence left my soul parched and lo! Souls never sign the death agreements , so unlike for generations, death couldn't come to my rescue

Yet I let one another epitaph be written and one another grave be dug

But the only thing I will miss is that one spade of soil that could have been your share of farewell

So dear moon, love as you do the stars , still they leave you alone in the most darkest of nights but nothing but a catastrophe faced little planet I am

No magnet for stars
Won't you tell me how you manage to bath me in your light
even after the lonely nights
And before I realize that you too were just an illusion, tell me-
Where shall I go?

17. The call

Have you ever felt it?
The call?
That of something
Not ordinary
A fine day you went to draw water
And saw him leave
As if drawn by some invisible thread
The man whom everyone avoided
The man who presence registered with no one
But he did what her heart longed to do
Leave
Or then also he who visited rarely
An unwelcome charming mysterious guest
But her heart welcomed him
The old wise man from lands unknown
He who knew what others knew not
Knew what lay out there
He who had had his call
The call that only some heeded to
He had been the finest of lads
But then no one knew what happened
Some say he had left for the jungles
He wanted something called adventure

They gasped at the alien
But she knew it
He had had his call
The call of the wild..

18. Insanity at the sea

The reality I found so difficult to find
They talked about a man of ship
That miniature in the fragile glass
When ghosts steered the lost ships
They partied under the damp branches
Uncomfortable ripples for the music
While I watched from the corner
They knew not of the treasures
They knew not of the chests
They knew not of the directions
And of the navigations they knew not
Aggression, rough ways, boiling tempers
The tea from the rusty teapots
The buns infested with seaweed
The gravy smelling of salty sickness
The matted hair adding on to the ranks
The greasy clothes to the sweaty labour
The adored flag they too great care of
Of the infested workers they couldn't care less
The differentiation lost directions
My work got mixed with the wages
The wages that were reduced to mere survival
But then you don't compliment survival

We polished the deck everyday
For the man in the navy to navigate
But that was the concept not the captain
For he was the man with the most matted hair
He was flea bitten and so were we
We whom the fleas bit for the recognition
And then I fall short of words
At a point when I don't know
This from that and that from this
What meddled with my brain?
A brain thankful for still being able to ask
It wasn't sea sickness
It wasn't the infested captain
It wasn't the rotting ship
It wasn't the directionless direction
It wasn't the dry water
It just was something

Something that I wondered was what
But it was and made sure of its existence
And it kept us enslaved and in awe
Of the ceaseless sea of the weird captain
We thought of leaving
But that held us back
Something that was unreal
Something that was an illusion
That frustrating force

That something that no one knew the name of
But just
Yeah ...that something....

19. Appreciation

Flour smeared clothes
Forehead supporting cherry mash streaks
Eyes twinkling, the perfect carved out slice
The enthusiastic gobble, the thankless departure
Her cataract veiled eyes pored hard
Blurred visions of sewing buttons
Thankless adornment of mended clothes
The offerings that never got small
Smiles that held no price tags
Gooey smiles that mimicked hope
So many things to express gratitude for
Though so little realization of it
The getting up on a beautiful morning
The first golden sun rays brushing the face
The breathing in of the free cold air
Catching the sweet chirping of the early birds
The very sweet thought of freedom
Freedom of going through the day fearlessly
The worrying about normal things
The necessary amount of stress
Whoever raised their hands
Raised hands not to ask for anything
Raised hands in appreciation

Raised hands to thank
Gratitude for the unnoticed
Gratitude for the little things

20. Fleeting fickle frivolity

A shadow flittering across a lane of mismatched cobblestones
. A shadow that calls nowhere home.
Tiptoeing on the many shades of ancient stones. An
unwanted shadow in a celebrated city. The messily
coloured blue framed window shows into a hurriedly put up
kitchen the mixed colours, an unexpected but
not unwanted bohemian look. The family dynamics even
more rugged than the soles of the rustic hippie's
shoes. The family even more tough than the Vikings of the
unsure past. The happy whiff of the freshly
brewed tea provides no welcome to the stranger at the
window. The rose bud covered latch uncovers the
hidden subtle thorns underneath . When no markets waited
in advance. No delicate draping cover the
exotic shaded faces. No eyes waiting for the one never seen
before. A stranger that calls a strange place as
home.
COMBAT— The streets support the ghosts of the children
that played there from dawn till dusk. Their
plays distinguishing no hour from the next. The shadow
kidnaps the ghosts, filling them in a sack and
heading towards the illusionary hosts. A sack full of
murderous wishes and zero tantrums. The fragile head

supporting mane of hair that tumbles down the archaic
architecture. Dissected golden glimmers of the
slanting sunshine sew an intricate canopy among the subtle
ecosystem. The cold damp, slimy shadow of the
dark brooding shadow. The so many times removed reality of
a nightmare. The charm of the golden locks
diminishing the unnoticeable negative effect. And still the
ghostly shadow steps lurk around the precisely
cut edges of the bright sunlight. An aged understanding a
wrinkled beauty basking in the blissful
meaningful little things laughs a toothless laugh as the silver
mopped head moves side to side in a jingling
frequency to dangling flashing tinkling loops underneath all
the glory and all the dazzle, the old soul, the
years have a deep imprint of the feeble shadow.

21. Abstract

Felt like the sun had decided to leave early
Some miles on foot, some on cloudy cabs
His checked cloth covered lunch
Too spicy, made in sizzling heat
Clocks started appearing in dreams too
So he was on time, well.. The clock showed so
I sat there, gazing through the mosaic panes
Lo! Through ether, through canopies
He never minded to share his warmth
Perfume less baths of sunshine, oh! The UVs
I wondered aimlessly, but then
When did wandering have a concrete aim
About life, about reason, about existence
Blaring of a machine, serving as an aid
The whispering of seas, the rustling of leaves
The chirping of avis, the music of lands
Now if the centre of the system is humble
Can't expect the mere disciples
To mimic the sacrifices too
My hands are tied with invisible ropes
My moment! Grab the fastest chariot
And let the horses wild and free
For waiting is the epitome of patience

Isn't it enough for the abstract?

22. Unscientific sciences

My strip of film, the Polaroid

Age scented memories, stunned capturing

The stolen colours from the rainbow

The china capturing it in varied shades

Brushing the still waters with my fingers

Beneath the layer, the moving creatures

The dazzling paper lights, blinding rays

The powders, pastes, the stuffed jars

The experience lend by the aged hands

The rugged stones, the threadbare carpets

The time spent to show the expertise

The blend of tales, spices and lazy sunshine

The remembrances on rainy days

The misty eyes, the wisps from the lonely coffee

The roughness of the wool, cold warmth

The nostalgic vibes from the clocks

The raw longing for the warm hands

The desire for the gone days

The cold classrooms, the chilly lectures of relativity

The dilations, the black holes, the space wraps

The emotions making you want to understand

The science for the sake of feelings...

23. Her

The bohemian hair jewellery entwined around my tresses
The sticky glitter decorating my nails in all shades
Made them imagine a girl in whom resided all sorts of happy,
careless and completely reckless spirits
She walked in a manner that mirrored the winds
Never touching anything yet feeling everything
She had her feet tucked in the wedges
Which when catching the rays from the sun
Shone like pieces of a broken mosaic mirror
Adding to the glitter of her turquoise eyes
Her smile had that magnetizing tint to it
But her own self defied all laws of physics
Though metaphysics could have been excused
She felt choked yet no one breathed so freely
She felt tied yet there was something in the way she moved
She was the most heartbroken but you
never saw a lively heart
Had she perfected the skill of living behind the mask?
Or was she so lifeless that nothing mattered anymore
Just going on with the flow and being a sheep
Or was her lifelessness a new way of life

24. Penning down the pain

If only my blood filled my inkpot

And my veins metamorphosed into fingers

Could I smooth my heart as my parchment

And pen down the wounds in the reddest of inks

I doubt they even sell in the most exotic streets of Kabul.

25. On the road

That frozen road watched from above
Unruly haired artist's master strokes
That bohemian art over your neck
That glowing tan, the dark scars
Those endless cars, those ceaseless drives
I hang on to the scent of fluttering hair
You crumpled the map, your lost direction
Felt your wild heart beating loud
We reached a city of unknowns
The normal amidst the mad
The hospitality had us hostage
Hostage to good drinks, weird foods
Memory losses, dizzy encounters
Left from a very different lane
And hit the tanning summer road
My blowing scarf felt chocking
My lungs grew branches of exotic fruits
My eyes- way too much liberating
And I wondered who drove the car
Whom did I leave behind?
The stranger that was my companion
The day is new, it is another
We don't succumb to pressures

Don't you remember we planned it?
Yeah, somewhere in a lost memory
So dive after three flips
When you hit the bottom
Let your bubbles guide you back
To your much earned gulp of air

26. Gaining gaps

Light came inside in an array of colours
Rectilinear propagations, ironed ends
But in chaos it hit me, tangled matters
That dripping of water from a broken tap
The tickling of the dominating ugly clock
The rustle of the too many fallen leaves
And them also the bicycle over them
Where lies the beauty? What matters?
The marshmallows roasting in the fire
The warmth of dry socks and the crackle
The security lend by the comforting arms
I heard the beauty of the crackling fire
But
The cold clingy damp foul freezing air
The marble feet over the rough gravel
The absence of even the ghost of presence
The leaves are not a golden bronze
The clock is not measuring the moments right
The water is not quenching the thirst
The bicycle man doesn't touch his hat now
Ask the dry throats, the deaf ears
Those whom the arms left alone
Those for whom the fire is too cold

But who even ever bothered
Bothered to ask....to understand
The light, oh yes! The colourful clown
Through the wound it finally entered

27. Where did I go?

I watched my moths getting tired
Stuck in that glass jar, shut tight
But they glowed, lightened up my place
And that was what mattered, only that
The cold air froze me, gnawing on me
The grate lay empty grey and cold
My firewood all wet, unable to warm up
My skin changed colours, my feelings too
Still it changed nothing, I couldn't get up
The fire was blazing like never before
I felt the warmth, felt the bias brewing
But it won't stop here, loving too hard
And then it burnt me, badly burnt me
I had my glass filled to the brim
With hers, his, theirs...confusing cocktails
The rain pattered hard, steel gray
The house finally caught fire
God! I had lost myself, my own self
That day I carved it all out
My worm bitten wood, my infested flesh
Now over the mantelpiece, below the chimney
That day grandfather clock goes on ticking
I watch it with a perspective, personal one

The times it showed me, the bravery of it
The panes won't resist, they never learnt
They let it all in, the chills the chilling chills
And they are the path finders, the navigators
They went deep down somewhere, way too deep
The surgeries they performed, the dissections
It stank of hurt, of betrayal and the worldly ways
Raven black robes on pearl white snow
And I ran away, ran like never before
For I wanted the sun inside me to rise
Wanted the shimmering rays to fill me
The place that welcomed everything
I wanted to seek my own self
And I never went back to where I lost it

28. We are healing courtesy: SARS CoV2

Something has changed! ”
"Don't you feel so?"
_ Mr. Otter, checking the territory!
"Darling! Is it really so?"
_Mrs Otter, too afraid to have a peep! "Aha!
"Aha! Daddy, see me floating
On a log, a god damn log!"
_ Baby Otter, the butterflies at the tree top
Three moist noses smell around hysterically
Reassuring whooshes seep in unhindered
"Beautiful things take time to sink in!"
_ Grandpa Otter, glasses sliding down his wise nose!
That something that nobody could point at
What is it?
Are the winds behaving differently today?
Air drunk with the elixir of youth
The waters? Aren't they less crowded?
Waters resting after the forced project It is raining cats and dogs
Waters revelling in waters
A celebration that was so thirsted for
That the parching now quenched the thirst

Mrs. Swan is thrilled for her babes

They are watching the gone time come alive

The historic history repeating itself

When the planet hired the honest maid

Oh! How she dusts it all off!

Go on! Have a laugh at yourselves!

Humility does wonders!

"Was our presence a passing thing?"

_The otter family rolling on the mat....

The perfect day oh!

"Do you know these moves?"

_The hippie dolphin doing the dance of the free!

But the wise penguin wonders why?

Is the pandemic over?

"Oh! Dear that must be it!"

_ Mrs Penguin, cries below from a lake!

The star strewn sky is ablaze tonight!

They are showing the news up above !

"It is Bald Eagle reporting live from the free studio.

Renowned Dr Nature has found the vaccine to

the Pandemic that has made the animal world suffer for times

immeasurable. The vaccine has been name as SARS COV2

And it has caged the humans like nothing before! Though it is

feared that if the humans get immune to it they might emerge

out to be even more brutal and filthier. But for now, it is a free

Planet! "

_ Mr. Eagle reports in a serious voice that is leaking with excitement!

"Someone blast off some damn it music!"

_ The lemur from Madagascar!

It is an old record when Ms. Panda was in her early youth

The days of the stardom flash before her eyes!

The unexpected retrospection!

The song is called "We are healing"!

And the music goes on and on

Filling the night air

With no humans to pollute it

With smug and smoke

"We need to save this planet, people!".

_ Invaders inside CFC laden rooms

"Baby! I know all too well how to save me!"

_ Earth with a swish of her green grasslands

What was here before us

Knows all too well

How to be here even after us!

_ Syed Nahida (An extremely troubled yet unapologetic invader)

29. Dry Blossom

The light wind made the branches come alive
It tapped on my window pane, knocking hard
The fact being quite strange that it confuses me
Was anyone home I wondered ? Was I there?
Sometimes basics get us muddled up, usually
Or maybe it is the curiosity to look underneath
Under so many things, so many feelings
Under so many faces, so many voices
I pressed the dried flowers in my hand softly
The harshness still not daring to creep in
They used to tell me that over thinking is bad
It ruins the facts, the reality, the real things
The child who tries his mum's makeup excitedly
The real purpose gets lost somehow at last
The mum got angry , her favourite kit was ruined
She beathed hard under the piled over quilt
What will keep her busy now? The day being over
So there it goes, the string of ifs, maybes, what ifs
Wait how many even had that thing cross their minds?
See I told you not to over think, the quilt suffocating
There was a child once who played with makeup
The mum laughed and took out the old camera
The papery skin, the bony fingers turned the crisp page

The day when you messed with the rainbow, remember
The ringing laughter, it remembered all too well
The knocking continued, you continued knocking
Was it you I wondered? A lot to wonder now
Was it the silence? The day silence knocked at my heart
I mistook it for you and it had come for a long stay
Now no knock gets registered, they come and go
I forgot you and now I remember you again
The silence a constant reminder, a pest
The crisp flowers continue to be stroked softly
As I wait for the blooming season of love....

30. And then I was gone

Forlorn flower beds in dreary weather
Were crowned my mirrors for the day
The ground no more felt cold now
We lost each other, it in me, me in it
But I will find myself some other day
It hung heavy in me, uninvited guest
My breath a prisoner to it, helpless
My epitome of contrast shone, shining
Weak wintery sunlight, hoping strongly
The bare branches still cherished it though
Like the kind word that made your day
Through the moist vision I observed
Blur, clear vision, changed places
I wondered whether I did it completely
Wondered whether I lived fully
Wondered whether I forgave everything
Wondered whether I cleared the doubts
Wondered I loved with everything I had
Wondered whether I comforted fully
Wondered whether I found the purpose
Wondered whether I had sorted the priorities
Wondered whether I had been available
Wondered whether I let it all go

The weak sunshine didn't give up
Who guaranteed my tomorrow?
What was I fighting for?
Did I think that before I went on war?
The clock on the tower went on
Tick..moment ..tick..another moment
On and on and on and on and on
But not both sides looked the same
One went on while the other ceased, full stop
The car had drove fast...like never before
Weak sun upon the forlorn graveyard
The clock on the tower watched on
They had assembled slowly, one then the other
They had come...it seemed by the look of it
The soil didn't make it possible to see
So the flowers were never smelt
The tears never seen, emotions unfelt
What if I had just let go... Foolishness
Each beat tears me down now, scratching
Disgust fills me up mixed with the blood
I don't know where your breath now resides
What is that place tell me...somehow
Would they allow us to meet there?
Behind the many heavy hearts
Was the heaviest one, nails biting skin
The tears frustrated him, the clothes choked
Now I don't see you, I had the chance

That day the soul had spoken strange
No let me see, what if I left without seeing
Without forgiving, without loving
What held me back then, the nails cut
But it bleeds even more than seen
Only if yesterday was today... the pain
Unexplainable pain, I fell on my knees
Wishing some soil opened for me too
The bloodshot eyes looked up at the sky
One more chance, give me yesterday
The clock on the old withering tower
Well....if only clocks could laugh

31. Stuck with being lonely

The leaves fall in a rhythmic swirl. An artistic shedding of all that which is spent. Many months have passed
and they showed me the different shades of loneliness. It is indeed a surprising fact that how an emotion
that is so loathed has a way of transforming into so many disguises.
There is a door that lets me see through another door at the end of the long dark corridor separating the
two entrances. The door frames a lady with a dropping head , a dampening aura. A lonely dandelion rests
beside her and the long peach painted chipped nails feel the obligation to turn the lonely-out-of-place-
flower at regular intervals. The frame has the two of them trapped.
An illusion of nature sets her mind free but the freedom somehow doesn't make it past this narrow door.
Her emotions are stuck in a loop.
The capturing of the soul rendering the flesh motionless

32. Tongue tied

The strange weird awkwardness prevails
When it was too hard to say anything
When you were left tongue tied
Emotions that defied descriptions
The crusts and troughs appeared all the same
The happiness that choked things
The boy who couldn't thank his mother enough
The gratitude that fell short of words
He owed her and owed her for life
Now that owing imprinted in a heart of bearing
The grief that never lessened whatsoever
The grief that couldn't be shared
The grief that fairy tale watered the flowers
Yet the grief that withered inside unknown
Then he asked her are you happy
So happy she was that she cried
And he felt sorry for everything
Mere agreement wasn't enough
And the explanation she wasn't capable of
So they let it be and letting be is disturbing
The time when he was so sorry
And said it a hundred times
So many times and then it didn't sound as a word

Words, words, words and yet not enough words
If only feelings accepted measurements
The scales the proofs they would always carry
But we felt short of expressions
And then we carried like that
Unexpressed emotions unsaid sayings
Suppressed feelings unfinished expressions
And then we are humans
Things are bound to be complicated
We don't meet completions
It would be strange if we did, wouldn't it be?

33. Things will turn out to
be all good

A cold steel gray washed over the witnessing sky
He drew the curtains yet again and watched
Watched the unpredictable sea, the roaring waves
The blaring radio had got it all wrong
No predicted news tamed the wild waves
And he waited, the unnecessary, unwanted wait
He knew how it was but then the hesitation
Push the raft, get going, the sea awaits you
Are you afraid of the sea? Where do you go then?
He watched on the wavering waves with wavering decisions
But then what the wavering needs is a contradiction by the
steady
A gust of chilling salty air hit him hard
The sea was fickle; it never shared its secrets
Like the day you decided to rest and lost the raft
And the sea decided to act like the dead
Oh! How it mirrored the still shining sky
The glistening sea that was never guilty of disturbances
But the shocked inhabitant of the old shack knew better
Knew better, repeated mistake is a conscious decision
The lost raft was found and pushed hard against the cold
Against wavering decision, against unpredictable weathers

Against freezing frostbites, against fickle innocent looking waters

Amidst the crashing waves something washed over the fearless

A detached moment, somewhere in a calm cosy cottage

A little boy waited for too many things, feared too much

And the not-too-much-remembering-Grandma went on knitting

And said "things will turn out to be all good...they always do"

And he simply believed her and knew better

34. Empathetic waters

I watched as the ocean stretches endlessly in front of me. The rough sand feels soothing under my feet, a reminder that I am alive. The roughness long forgotten. The washing waves contrast to the still sky. I haven't stepped in the waters yet I feel like I am drowning. I spot some driftwood nearby. Some fresh wood just out of the wet waters and yet some bleached wood too. They scream out a contrast and my inner frequencies just tune in. The waters start to lull me after some silent moments and the gulls I hear out crystal clear. The epitome of sensitiveness. It is rippling noise outside, calm unmoving on the surface and a storm inside. It starts to drizzle. I know a prediction. Surprisingly yet more unsurprisingly I don't run for a shelter. My hair now hangs down in drenched rat tails. My raw red hands sweep it back. My motions calm yet swift, calculated yet disturbed. There is no time to wonder, no time to analyse and nothing to think. The only thought that surfaces is that of depth. And the deep I fear to think about. The waters now watch on with changed colours. Maybe I can leave everything in these salty airs here and come back tomorrow... The

waters witnessed as they had for centuries and the sand buried
as it had for centuries I thought the waters
understand so I came

35. The blue jackal

She smelt it on her very first step
That whiff of terror that hung there
Enveloping every single thing present
The creaking houses reeked of it
They closed the windows on her
A stranger from a strange land
They feared the strange, the unknown
The sun appeared odd, watery, and sodden
The water didn't let itself to be drunk
The stench was sharp like rusted blood
The children huddled to watch her
A novelty scanned with deep shadowed eyes
The smiles never returned
The greetings got stuck in midair
Helping neighbours didn't exist
A loner amidst the cold cowering crowd
The silence screamed the secret
Yet the movements could get no more suspicious
An almost entitlement of contamination
But that was not to stop anyone
Investigations feeding on the suspicions
And as it always was the case
The blue jackal ruled them all

Packing the remaining belongings she wondered
About the crackling fire and her grandma
The stories that gave her sleepless nights
And then about the many reeking houses
With their fires and telltale grandmothers

36. The vicious circle

It is us, two girls, two pods in a pea. We work a lot. Our mum brought us two scarves. Tapestries of cheery springs and cold blood murder depicting classic art pieces. As the cock crows we roll out of our humble beds and splash ice-cold water on our faces. There isn't much that comes in the house, it is a meagre income, some shillings and even lesser notes tied in a bundle that mother cares with all her being but the food on the table reflects a different story altogether. Can't call it a feast exactly but it isn't a poor man's meal either. Fresh eggs from the coop, the jam that mother spent the whole day making, freshly baked bread that was worked for in the fields.

But the dedication doesn't always hover around. It is an amalgamation of crusts and troughs. At times the smeared flour decorates the flushed faces, the cherry dipped tips are licked with relish, the baked bread bathes us in an aroma of accomplishment. But at other times monotony rides heavy on our backs, the kitchen - a living breathing monster that has managed to capture us inside a snake devouring its tail.

We climb up to the attic and open the chipped creaking window and far away we can see a row of mountains. We have never been there, don't even know the name but there is a winding road that leads up to there.

We are packing our bags tonight. Two bags for us two girls. Let the road dictate further...

37. Completion

The flames raised high, the smoke higher

I inhaled mouthfuls of my routine

The dirt building in my metamorphosis

I learned to search for my time in the shadows

I dreamt of rough soil between my fingers

The water stained with mud woke me up

The remembrance of the grooves in the trees

The partition in the colours, in the winds

I recalled, I remembered, I faced it everyday

The days that came earlier irritated me

My hands left raw with harsh scrubbing

Then the soil rested in the finger nails

It got nostalgic with my passing shadows

A leaf to my identity, raw roughness

The turban was stained green, the hands brown

Processed cane juice, my treat for days

We matched now, the bodies, the endurances

And then when we prayed, the real connections

My lips to the soil, my ears to the brook

I don't hide from the firmaments

But there were things that were strange

I fell in love with the rough soil

The night troubled me I thought

Realisation knocked at my trap then

The trap I feared, the ceilings haunted me

The shirt stuck, the veins throbbed

Forgotten carved woods, feared hinges

I never slept more soundly, more peacefully

Old friends my winds, then also the open skies

The wind sang lullabies, the stars watched on

The leaves fanned, the soil hugged

My nails scratched the soil while I slept

My beloved I tickle it, it feels loved

Forgetting had made it hostile

The brushing makes it feel loved

I don't fear the insides now, how could I

It whispers to me in the dark nights

The day when I will finally live in it

But for now I burn fires

The blending colours, the murmuring

The grooves, the roughness, the lullabies

But then also the shadows and more shadows

My heart rejoices, the muddy water in my veins

But they won't leave me alone though

I don't like the cane juice now, the stained turban

They watch with bulged eyes, strange creatures

They even fear the soil in my nails sometimes

They pass too fast sometimes, restlessness

The spotless veils, the empty laughter

The view watching in the holiday season

I laugh secretly in my dear nights

I have my beloved with me

And they pity me, strange understandings

Salty soils, pressed lips, forehead grooves

Things are getting stranger now

So last night the winds whispered

And I never have to scratch anymore

I am complete now, he called me

I live in it now

And the stained turban is still searching…

38. Seasonal depression

There are waves of pastel purples, sea greens and ocean blues in this haven of yours. As you surface from this minimalistic resting wooden layout of yours , as you adjust the blocks on your wall the warm sunlight enters unasked and conquers your territory. Was it supposed to make you happy? These torn wallpaper musty mustard walls of your narrow corridor lead you to a unhappy lay out on a now revolting pale tablecloth. These sad eggs that you feel guilty of eating now, this milk that has that inextricable sour tint to it now, this no better than burnt rubber bread.

You can't be bothered about making any timetable. You can't be bothered about having any plans. You kind of know beforehand it will all fail anyways. This season won't let anything succeed. This season had made you into Mr. Mole of the underground hole. Depressed, dirt drenching Mr. Mole. The hate makes you feel guilty but you can't help it. You stand under the shower getting drenched in waters of helplessness and revolt. A selection from the guillotine of hung clothes, they aren't big enough to hide you anymore. They are having parties out there. Summer water parties. This combination of words is your personal death sentence. And then this dread dawns upon you and you rush to shut the windows, to draw the curtains to block all that is lively and warm outside. This terrorizing notice from your school calls you out. You cry and curse, pray and pant, dread and drown but it is like nobody has the time to register your drama. It is almost as if it is unnoticeable. In your heart you carry all the grudge as you step in the enemy territory. You are at a war with the world. Today you hate everyone. Can't they even let you hide peacefully.

No they won't.

You have got to merge.

Rip your heart out

Throw it away

And walk on

Walk on my dummy

Walk in the fresh summer air

The world is calling you...

39. Self appointments

You could see the glint in the cracked glass, then a flicker and then all that was lit vanishes into pitch darkness. The day had dawned with a deep purple streak across the periwinkle blue sky. The piles of rust ridden films are being enveloped with a stale air that makes them unwatchable. The cinnamon shaded floor is strewn with too many crumpled papers to count. The courtyard is a busy cluttered painting of a casual artist. The floral shirt is a everyday party casual wear with deep stubborn coffee stains. It has been pinned with grandma's old plastic pink clips and is flying in the breeze like the free bird it is, carefree dirty laundry. A tin tub stands overturned in the corner near the fence overflowing with gleaming corn and some unrecognisable brown seeds. The hens are clustered around the feast, a clash of pecks and pokes.

Last Tuesday a small gathering was held in the garden and everything looked new, strange and mismatched. The energies won't synchronize, the lyrics won't match, the conversation won't fall in sequence. It was a mess. It was novelty. It was an unwanted, imperfect perfection. There had been the dragging of too many chairs and when the occupations rose to unmanageable heights, overturned tubs did the job equally well. The stout lady whose apron gave off strong whiffs of all that was cooked and cleaned ushered all her six lads and all were seated down on the huge wicker basket. The little beady eyes searching for the promised feast. The table was the epitome of fuss and feasts. Chickens marinated with some lost oil of the long lost fields overlooked by living-in-threat chickens, fuzzy grape and fizzy pumpkin juices, sautéed vegetables of all imaginable colours, lopsided cherry and berry strewn cakes were all laid on the lavender printed tablecloth. A clash of teaspoons and forks and the interference of small chubby hands. By the end of the meal all that remained were the many stains, blue from the berries, red from the cherries, brown from cokes and yellow from the egg yolks. The guests left with their lads and the host carried in the ladles. Scrubbing the too many dishes, washing the table cloth that had met brutal treatment, cleaning the cluttered courtyard took the whole next day. There was hardly a moment of rest. And that was about the Tuesday and the Wednesday that followed.

That is how the days are here. Filled with self appointed appointments and the unenthusiastic cleaning afterwards. The days are vast and they welcome all that fills the space between the energetic dawn to the drowsing dusk.

9 7 9 8 8 8 7 0 4 7 3 4 8